THE USBORNE PICTURE DICTIONARY

Felicity Brooks

Designer and modelmaker: Jo Litchfield

Design and additional illustrations by
Mike Olley and Brian Voakes

Photography by Howard Allman

Contents

Managing Designer: Mary Cartwright
Americanization Editor: Carrie Seay
Editorial Assistant: Fiona Patchett

Additional models by Les Pickstock, Barry Jones, Stef Lumley, Karen Krige and Stefan Barnett

With thanks to Staedtler for providing the Fimo® material for models.
Bruder® toys supplied by Euro Toys and Models Ltd.

SCHOLASTIC INC.
New York Toronto London Auckland Sydney
Mexico City New Delhi Hong Kong Buenos Aires

Using your dictionary

The words in a dictionary are in the same order as the letters of the alphabet. This means words that begin with A come first, then words that begin with B, and so on. In this dictionary there are many things on each page to help you to find the word you are looking for.

This letter in a blue square shows the first letter of the words on that page.

This word shows the first word on the page.

This word shows the last word on the page.

The words that you can look up are shown in blue. You can find out about the words in parentheses on page 4.

Don't forget that in a dictionary you read down the page in columns. In most other books you read across.

Sometimes the same word appears twice with little numbers next to it. This shows that the same word can be used in two very different ways.

If you forget the order of the letters in the alphabet, look at the bottom of any page.

The blue letter also shows the first letter of the words on that page.

How to find a word

1 Think of the letter the word starts with. "Stone" starts with an "s", for example.

2 Look through the dictionary until you have found the "s" pages.

3 Think of the next letter of the word. Look for words that begin with "st".

4 Now look at all the "st" words until you find your word.

Can you find?

For practice, you could try looking up these words:

bat

street

lion

hill

wash

jacket

cake

music

Alphabet game

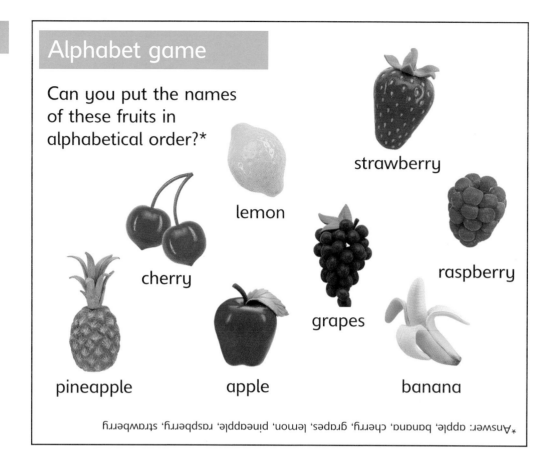

Can you put the names of these fruits in alphabetical order?*

strawberry

lemon

raspberry

cherry

grapes

pineapple

apple

banana

*Answer: apple, banana, cherry, grapes, lemon, pineapple, raspberry, strawberry

Looking at a word

When you have looked up a word, here are some of the things you can find out.

You can find out what a word means.

You can find out how to spell a word.

know (knew, known)
1. If you know someone, you have met them before.

These children know each other.

You can see how you can use a word.

2. have something in your mind

You can see if a word can mean different things.

A picture tells you more about a word.

hippopotamus
(also called a hippo)
a very big animal with short legs and thick skin

You can also find out if a word can be shortened.

hen (also called a chicken)
a bird that farmers keep

This tells you another word for the same thing.

Net²
a short name for the Internet

You can find out if a word is short for something.

know (knew, known)
1. If you know someone, you have met them before.

Turn the page to find out about words in parentheses.

3

Talking about the past

"Doing" words, such as "walk", "smile" and "eat" are called verbs. When you use a verb to talk about the past (the time before now), you usually just add "ed" or "d" to the end of the word:

Danny likes to walk to school.

Yesterday Danny walk**ed** to school.

Danny has walk**ed** to school every day this week.

My baby can smile.

She smile**d** yesterday.

My baby has smile**d** a lot this week.

For some verbs, you don't add "d" or "ed", but another ending to talk about the past. Some verbs change completely:

Robert likes to **eat** pasta.

Yesterday he **ate** pasta.

He has **eaten** pasta every day this week.

In this dictionary, you can see these changes in parentheses ( ) after the word:

eat (ate, eaten)

Comparing words

"Describing" words, such as "small", "expensive" and "good" are called adjectives. When you use an adjective to compare things, you usually just add "er" or "est" to the end of the word:

A horse is small**er** than an elephant, but a mouse is the small**est**.

For some adjectives, instead of adding "er" or "est", you say "more" or "most" before the word:

A car is **more** expensive than a bicycle.

A truck is the **most** expensive.

You must be **more** careful.

Sara is the **most** careful.

For a very few adjectives, you don't add "er" or "est", or "more" or "most", but change the whole word:

This cake is **good**.

This cake is **better**.

This cake is the **best**.

In this dictionary, you can see these unusual words in parentheses ( ) after the word:

good (better, best)

More than one

"Naming" words, such as "goat", "sheep", "mouse" and "child" are called nouns. When you use a noun to talk about more than one thing, you usually add an "s" to the end of the word:

one goat   two goat**s**

one house   two house**s**

If the word already ends with an "s", you add "es" to the end instead:

one cross   two cross**es**

For a very few nouns, you don't add an "s" or "es" to the end, but keep the word exactly the same:

one sheep   two **sheep**

For a few nouns you add a completely different ending:

one child   two child**ren**

For some nouns, you don't change the ending, but you change the whole word:

one mouse   two **mice**

one goose   two **geese**

In this dictionary, you can see these unusual words in parentheses ( ) after the word:

child (children)

actor

someone who pretends to be another person and acts in a play

add

1. find the answer to a sum like this one:

$$8 + 2 =$$

2. put something with something else

Billy's adding two blocks.

address

words that show where someone lives

Oliver Muncher
233 Grub Avenue
Tulsa OK 74146

adult

a grown-up person

Minnie's dad is an adult.

afraid

If you are afraid, you think something is scary or bad.

Maddy is afraid of spiders.

after

If something happens after something else, it happens later.

Sacha

Sacha goes after Suki.

Suki

afternoon

the part of the day after the morning

3 o'clock in the afternoon

age

how old you are

Olivia

Joshua

Ben

Can you guess Olivia's age?

air

what we all breathe

A balloon floats in the air.

alone

not with other people

Katie's alone in the bathtub.

alphabet

all the letters you use to write words, put in a special order:

*abcdefghijklm
nopqrstuvwxyz*

ambulance

a special van that takes sick people to the hospital

a b c d e f g h i j k l m n o p q r s t u v w x y z

amount

how much there
is of something

a large
amount of
pasta

ankle

the part of your body that
joins your leg to your foot

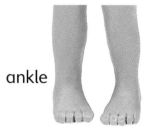

ankle

apple

a round fruit with red, green
or yellow skin

angel

a messenger sent from
heaven

answer

what you say or write when
someone asks you a question

Question: Which animal says
              "meow"?

Answer: A cat

arm

the part of your body
between your shoulder
and hand

angry

If you are angry, you feel
upset and want to shout.

ant

a very small insect

arrive

get to where you are going

The bus has just arrived.

animal

something that lives, moves
and breathes

ape

a large animal with long
arms and no tail

An orangutan is an ape.

art

something such as a painting
or drawing, that someone
has made

a b c d e f g h i j k l m n o p q r s t u v w x y z

6

artist
someone who draws or paints or makes other pieces of art

ask
1. say that you want to know something

2. say that you want something

She is asking for strawberries.

asleep
sleeping

astronaut
someone who goes into space

baby
a very young child

back¹
the part of your body between your neck and bottom

back²
the part farthest from the front of something

This boy is sitting at the back of the bus.

bad (worse, worst)
1. naughty

a bad dog

2. not good or not good to eat

a bad apple

bag
something you use to hold or carry things

bake
cook food, such as bread or cake, in an oven

Oliver is going to bake some muffins.

baker
someone who makes and sells bread and cakes

balance
keep your body or something steady so it does not fall

This clown can balance on one hand.

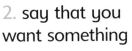

a b c d e f g h i j k l m n o p q r s t u v w x y z

bald

Someone who is bald has no hair on his head.

ball

1. a round thing that you use for games

2. a big party where people dance

ballerina

a woman who does a kind of dancing called ballet

balloon

a thin, rubber bag that gets bigger when you blow into it

banana

a long, curved fruit with a yellow skin

band

a group of people who play music together

bang

a sudden, loud noise

bank

1. a place where people keep money safe

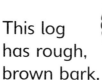

2. the edge of a river or stream

bar

1. a long, thin piece of metal or wood

2. a block of something

a bar of soap

bare

If you are bare, you have no clothes on.

bark[1]

the hard skin that covers a tree trunk

This log has rough, brown bark.

bark[2]

When a dog barks, it makes a loud noise in its throat.

Woof woof!

a b c d e f g h i j k l m n o p q r s t u v w x y z

barn *to* bed

barn

a large farm building for animals, straw or machines

base

the bottom part of something

a lamp with a yellow base

basket

something you use to hold or carry things

bat

1. a small, furry animal with wings

2. a kind of stick that you use to hit a ball

bathtub

something you fill with water and sit in to wash yourself

beach

land by the sea with sand or stones on it

playing on the beach

beak

the hard outside part of a bird's mouth

Toucans have big beaks.

bean

a long, thin vegetable, or the seeds inside it

bear

a big, wild animal with thick fur

beard

the hair on a man's chin

beautiful

very nice to look at, listen to or smell

a beautiful cake

bed

something you lie on to sleep or rest

a b c d e f g h i j k l m n o p q r s t u v w x y z

bedroom
a room you sleep in

before
If something happens before something else, it happens first.

Suki goes before Sacha.

Sacha

Suki

below
Something that is below something else is under it or lower than it.

The kitten is below the wood.

bee
a yellow and black insect that can fly. Some bees make honey.

begin (began, begun)
start to do something

Sam began to yawn.

belt
a long strip of plastic, leather or cloth that you wear around your tummy

beetle
a shiny insect with hard outside wings

behind
Something that is behind something else is at the back of it.

The kitten is behind the flowerpot.

beside
Something that is beside something else is next to it.

The kitten is beside the flowerpot.

beetroot (beetroot)
a round, dark red vegetable

belong
Something that belongs to you is yours.

The book belongs to Suzie.

between
Something that is between two things is in the middle of them.

The kitten is between the flowerpots.

a b c d e f g h i j k l m n o p q r s t u v w x y z

bib

something that a baby wears around its neck to keep its clothes clean

birthday

the date that you were born

a birthday party

boat

something that floats and can carry people and things across water

bicycle

a machine with two wheels, that you can ride

bite (bit, bitten)

use your teeth to cut into something

body

Your body is every part of you.

some parts of the body

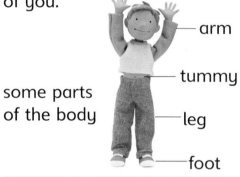

— arm

— tummy

— leg

— foot

big

large; not small

a big elephant

blanket

a thick cover that you can put on a bed

bone

the hard, white parts inside your body or inside an animal's body

Patch is gnawing a toy bone.

bird

an animal that has a beak, wings and feathers

blow (blew, blown)

1. make air come out of your mouth

2. When the wind blows, it moves the air.

book

something that you read that has pages attached inside a cover

a b c d e f g h i j k l m n o p q r s t u v w x y z

boot
a tall shoe that covers your foot and ankle

bowl
a kind of round, deep plate that holds food

brave
not afraid to do something scary

a brave firefighter

bottle
something made of glass or plastic that holds liquids

box
something made of cardboard, wood or plastic that you can keep things in

bread
a food made from flour and baked in an oven

bottom[1]
the part of your body that you sit on

boy
a child who is not a girl

break (broke, broken)
make something split into pieces or stop working

bottom[2]
the lowest part of something

The kitten is at the bottom of the stairs.

branch
part of a tree that grows from the trunk

breakfast
the first meal of the day

breakfast foods

a b c d e f g h i j k l m n o p q r s t u v w x y z

breathe

suck air through your nose or mouth and send it out again

Divers carry air to breathe underwater.

brush

something you use to tidy your hair, to clean your teeth or for painting

building

a place with walls and a roof

This building has ten floors.

bridge

something built over a road, river or railroad tracks so that people can get across

bucket

something you use to hold or carry things, such as sand or water

bump

knock into something or someone by mistake

Mr. Bun bumped into a dog.

bright

If a color or light is bright, it is strong and easy to see.

a bright yellow car

bug

an insect or other very small animal

burger

a round, flat piece of meat that you usually eat on a bun

bring (brought, brought)

take someone or something with you

Jack brought his letter to mail.

build (built, built)

make something by putting parts together

Billy is building a pyramid.

burn (burned, burned)

1. ruin or hurt something or someone with fire or heat

Dad burned the burgers.

2. be on fire

a b c d e f g h i j k l m n o p q r s t u v w x y z

bus

a big thing on wheels that can carry a lot of people

bush

a big plant with lots of branches. Bushes are smaller than trees.

a bush

a tree

busy

If you are busy, you have lots of things to do.

Mr. Bun is busy in the kitchen.

butcher

someone who sells meat

butter

a yellow food made from milk

butterfly

an insect with four large wings

button

a small, round thing that you use to fasten clothes

buy (bought, bought)

pay money for something so that you can have it

café

a place with tables and chairs where you can buy and eat snacks and drinks

Café Delargo

cage

a box or room with bars, for an animal

cake

a sweet, soft food that is baked in an oven

calf

a young cow

a cow and a calf

a b c d e f g h i j k l m n o p q r s t u v w x y z

call *to* castle

call

1. shout to someone or a pet so that they come to you

Come here!

2. give someone or something a name

camel

a large animal with one or two humps

camera

something you use to take photographs

camp

live in a tent for a short time

candle

a lump of wax with a string through the middle

cap

a soft hat with a round part at the front that shades your eyes

car

a big thing that people drive. It has four wheels and goes on roads.

card

something that you send to people at special times

carpet

a thick cover that is attached to the floor

This room has blue carpet.

carrot

a long, orange vegetable

carry

hold something and take it with you

Aggie is carrying some flowers.

castle

a big, strong building with high, stone walls

a b c d e f g h i j k l m n o p q r s t u v w x y z

cat

a furry animal with a long tail

cave

a big hole in a mountain or cliff, or under the ground

There's a bear in this cave.

chair

a seat with a back, made for one person to sit on

catch (caught, caught)

1. get a hold of something that is moving

Jack caught the ball.

2. get on a bus, train or plane

CD (short for compact disc)

a round piece of plastic with music or information stored on it

chalk

soft white or colored sticks that you can use for writing and drawing

caterpillar

a small, long animal that will turn into a butterfly or moth

center

the middle part of something

The fruit is in the center of the table.

chase

run after a person or animal to try to catch them

Jack and Polly are chasing the dogs.

cauliflower

a big vegetable with green leaves and a white middle

cereal

a kind of food that you eat with milk for breakfast

cheap

not costing much

Everything in this shop is very cheap.

a b c d e f g h i j k l m n o p q r s t u v w x y z

cheese
a food made from milk

chicken (also called a hen)
1. a bird that farmers keep

2. a kind of meat that comes from a chicken

choose (chose, chosen)
pick the things that you want

Billy can't decide which to choose.

chef
someone who cooks the food in a restaurant

child (children)
a young boy or girl

city
a very big town where a lot of people live and work

cherry
a small, round fruit with a pit in the middle

chin
the part of your face below your mouth

class
a group of people who learn together

chick
a very young chicken or other bird

a hen with five chicks

chocolate
a sweet food used to make cakes, candy and drinks

classroom
a special room where people have lessons

a b c d e f g h i j k l m n o p q r s t u v w x y z

clean[1]
take the dirt off something

clean[2]
not dirty

The boy in the middle is the only one with clean clothes.

climb
move up or down something high or tall

The firefighter is climbing up the ladder.

clock
something that shows the time

close[1] (say "kloze")
shut something

Danny is going to close the door.

close[2] (say "klose")
near

Bill and Ben are standing close together.

clothes
things that you wear

cloud
white or gray shapes that you see floating in the sky

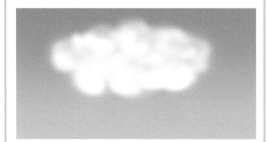

clown
someone who wears funny clothes and does tricks to make people laugh

coat
something you wear to keep you warm when you go outside

coffee
a hot, brown drink made from roasted coffee beans

coin
a small, round piece of metal money

Pete has two coins in his hand.

a b c d e f g h i j k l m n o p q r s t u v w x y z

cold *to* crash

C

cold[1]

an illness that makes you cough and sneeze a lot

Helen has a bad cold.

cold[2]

not hot or warm

Sam is wearing gloves because it is cold.

color

Red, green, yellow and blue are all colors.

comb

something made from metal or plastic that you use to tidy your hair

come (came, come)

1. move towards somebody or something

The clown comes into the house.

2. arrive
What time does the bus come?

computer

a machine that stores words, pictures and numbers and can send messages

cook

heat food to make it ready to eat

Dad is cooking pancakes.

copy

do the same as someone

Sally is copying Polly.

country[1]

a part of the world with its own name, people and laws

This map shows the countries of Africa.

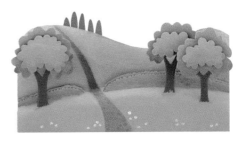

country[2]

the land outside towns and cities

cow

a big farm animal. Most milk comes from cows.

crash

hit something suddenly and make a loud noise

This car has crashed into a tree.

a b c d e f g h i j k l m n o p q r s t u v w x y z

crawl
move on your hands and knees

crayon
a colored pencil or a pencil made from wax

creep (crept, crept)
move very quietly and slowly

crocodile
a big animal with sharp teeth and a long tail

cross[1]
a mark made of two lines

cross[2]
go from one side to the other

Danny is crossing the road.

crown
a special gold or silver hat that a king or queen wears

cry
let tears fall from your eyes. You cry when you are hurt or unhappy.

cucumber
a long, green vegetable that you eat in salads

cup
something that you drink from. A cup usually has a handle.

cut (cut, cut)
use a knife or scissors to divide something into pieces

cycle
ride a bicycle

Sara cycles to school.

a b c d e f g h i j k l m n o p q r s t u v w x y z

dance
move your body to music

Steff and Laura are dancing.

dangerous
If something is dangerous, it may kill or hurt you.

Some snakes are dangerous.

dark
1. When it is dark, there is no light.

2. not pale or light

dark blue paint

date
the day and month when something happens

What's the date today?

day
1. the time when it is light outside

2. the 24 hours between one midnight and the next

dear
a word that you use at the beginning of a letter

Dear Ben,
Thank you v the lovely very usef

Dear Emily,
Thank you very much for the invitation to your party on June 26th.
I would love to come.
Sam xxx

deep
going down a long way

The digger is digging a deep hole.

deer
a big animal that can move quickly. Male deer have big horns called antlers.

delicious
very nice to eat or drink

Jack's sandwich is delicious.

dentist
someone who takes care of your teeth

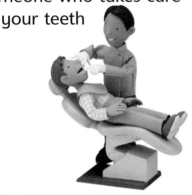

desert
very dry land where not many plants can grow

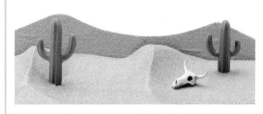

desk
a kind of table that you sit at to read, write or use a computer

a b c d e f g h i j k l m n o p q r s t u v w x y z

dictionary

a book of words. It tells you what words mean and how to spell them.

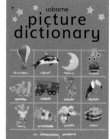

a picture dictionary

die

When someone or something dies, they stop living.

I forgot to water my plant and it died.

different

not the same

The twins are wearing different colors.

difficult

not easy to do

It's difficult to take care of two babies at the same time.

dig (dug, dug)

make a hole in the ground

digger

a big machine that can dig holes and move earth

dinner

a name for the biggest meal of the day

dinosaur

an animal that lived a long time ago. Some dinosaurs were enormous.

dirty

covered with mud, food or other stains

disappear

If something disappears, you cannot see it any more.

Polly's dog has disappeared.

dive

jump into water with your hands and head first

diver

someone who wears special clothes to swim underwater

a b c d e f g h i j k l m n o p q r s t u v w x y z

do *to* dream

do (did, done)

1. make something

Jenny is doing a jigsaw puzzle.

2. finish something

dolphin

a smart animal that lives in the sea. Dolphins are not fish.

dragon

a monster in stories that has a long tail and wings and breathes out fire

doctor

someone who helps sick people get better

donkey

an animal that looks like a small horse with long ears

draw (drew, drawn)

make a picture with a pen, pencil or crayons

dog

an animal that people keep as a pet or to do work

door

something you use to get into a room, building, car or cupboard

drawing

a picture someone has made with a pen, pencil or crayons

doll

a toy that looks like a small person

down

from a higher place to a lower one

This arrow points down.

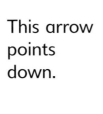

dream

a story that you see and hear while you are sleeping

a b c d e f g h i j k l m n o p q r s t u v w x y z

dress¹
something that girls and women wear

Anya is wearing a red dress with white flowers.

dress²
put on clothes

drink (drank, drunk)
swallow water or another liquid because you are thirsty

drive (drove, driven)
make a car, bus or other machine go somewhere

Mick is driving a dump truck.

drop¹
a tiny bit of water or another liquid

drop²
let something fall

Ellie has dropped her cake.

drum
a musical instrument that you hit with sticks or your hands

dry¹
take the water off or out of something or someone

Anna is drying herself with a towel.

dry²
not wet or damp

These clothes are dry.

duck
a bird that lives near water and can swim

duckling
a young duck

This duck has three ducklings.

dull
1. not very bright

a dull color

2. not very interesting

a dull story

a b c d e f g h i j k l m n o p q r s t u v w x y z

Ee eagle *to* e-mail

eagle
a big bird with sharp claws and a curved beak

easy
not hard or difficult to do

$$1 + 1 = ?$$

an easy sum

elbow
one of the two bony parts in the middle of your arms that make them bend

ear
a part of your body that you use to hear

eat (ate, eaten)
put food in your mouth and chew and swallow it

electricity
something that makes lights, televisions, computers and other things work

Electricity comes through wires to make a television work.

early
If you are early, you arrive sooner than someone expected.

Lucy arrived at the party early.

edge
the part along the side or end of something

The crayon is on the edge of the table.

elephant
a very big, gray animal, with a long nose called a trunk

Earth
1. the planet that we live on

2. earth
the stuff that plants grow in

egg
a smooth, oval thing that may contain a baby bird, fish or insect.
We often eat cooked hens' eggs.

e-mail
a message that you can send from one computer to another

Polly is sending an e-mail to her friend.

a b c d e f g h i j k l m n o p q r s t u v w x y z

empty

with nothing in it

This jar is empty.

end

the last part of something

the end of a TV film

enjoy

If you enjoy something, you like doing it.

Molly enjoys singing.

enormous

very big

Whales are enormous.

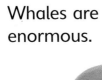

envelope

a paper cover for a letter or card

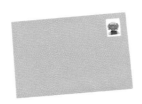

equal

If things are equal, they are the same.

Sally and Amy have equal amounts of sand.

escape

get away from somewhere

Jack's cat escaped from his arms and ran away.

even

An even number is a number that you can divide by two.

The bunny is jumping on even numbers.

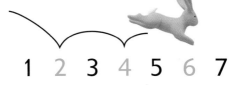

1 2 3 4 5 6 7

evening

the part of the day between the afternoon and night

The sun sets in the evening.

expensive

If something is expensive, it costs a lot of money.

15

4

Which toy is more expensive?

explain

make something clear so other people will understand it

Mr. Levy is explaining how to do these sums.

2+3 =
5+4 =
8+5 =

eye

a part of your body that you use to see

a b c d e f g h i j k l m n o p q r s t u v w x y z

face
the front part of your head

a happy face

facing
looking toward someone or something

These giraffes are facing each other.

fact
something that is true

It's a fact that little babies sleep a lot.

fairy
a tiny person, in stories, with wings

fall (fell, fallen)
go down to the ground suddenly

The clown fell in a pink pie.

far
a long way

The pet store isn't far from the butcher's store.

farm
a place where a farmer keeps animals and grows food

farmer
someone who has a farm

fast
If someone or something is fast, they move very quickly.

Eric can ski very fast.

fat
with a big, round body

a fat cat

feed (fed, fed)
give food to a person or animal

feel (felt, felt)
1. touch something to find out more about it

2. If you feel happy, for example, that is how you are at the time.

a b c d e f g h i j k l m n o p q r s t u v w x y z

fence

a kind of outdoor wall made from wood or wire

few

not many

Becky only has a few strawberries.

field

a big piece of land where people grow plants or keep animals

fight (fought, fought)

When people fight, they try to hurt each other.

The children are fighting.

fill

put so much into something that there is no space for any more

Ivan has filled his wheelbarrow with sand.

find (found, found)

see or get something that has been lost

Megan found the crayons.

finger

one of the five long, thin parts at the end of your hand

finish

come to the end of something

Danny has almost finished his juice.

fire

heat and bright light that comes from something that is burning

fire engine

a kind of truck that carries all the things firefighters need to put out fires

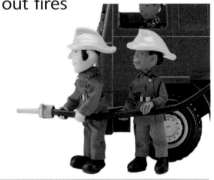

firefighter

someone whose job is to put out fires

first

before all the others

Jenny is first in the line.

a b c d e f g h i j k l m n o p q r s t u v w x y z

fish¹ (fish)

an animal that lives and breathes underwater. We eat some kinds of fish.

fish²

use a net or a rod to try to catch fish

fit¹ (fit, fit)

If clothes fit you, they are the right size.

Jenny's sweater doesn't fit. It's too big for her.

fit²

healthy and strong

Alice plays tennis to keep fit.

fix

repair something that is broken

Eve is fixing her doll.

flag

a piece of cloth with a special pattern on it. Each country has its own flag.

the French flag

flat

without any curves or bumps in it

Mr. Clack is sawing a flat piece of wood.

float

1. stay on the surface of water

2. stay up in the air

flood

a lot of water that covers ground which is usually dry

floor

the part of a room that you walk on

The floor is covered in toys and clothes.

flour

a powder usually made from wheat that you use to make bread and cakes

flower

a part of a plant. Flowers are often bright colors.

a b c d e **f** g h i j k l m n o p q r s t u v w x y z

fly[1]

a small insect with see-through wings

fly[2] (flew, flown)

move through the air

Birds can fly.

foal

a young horse

a foal   a horse

fold

bend one part of something over another part

food

what you eat to stay healthy

foot (feet)

a part of your body at the end of your leg

forest

a place where a lot of trees grow close together

forget (forgot, forgotten)

If you forget something, you don't remember it.

Jan has forgotten which way to go.

fork

something that you use to eat with. It has three or four points.

fox

a wild animal that looks a little like a dog. Foxes have long, bushy tails.

free

1. If something is free, you don't have to pay for it.

2. allowed to go where you want or do what you want

freeze (froze, frozen)

become very cold

When water freezes, it turns into ice.

a b c d e **f** g h i j k l m n o p q r s t u v w x y z

freezer

a machine that keeps food very cold so that it does not go bad

fresh

1. If food is fresh, it has just been made or picked and is not bad.

Mrs. Martin sells fresh fruit.

2. If air is fresh, it is clean.

friend

someone that you like and who likes you

Ellie's friends are coming to her party.

friendly

If you are friendly, you like to meet other people and are kind to them.

Marco is very friendly.

frog

a small animal that lives near water. It has big back legs for jumping.

front

the part that comes first or that you see first

front door of a car

fruit

something such as an apple or orange that grows on a bush or tree

fry

cook something in oil or butter

Dad is frying some eggs.

full

If something is full, it cannot hold any more.

Greg's cart is full of groceries.

fun

If something is fun, you enjoy it and it makes you happy.

Ben and Suki are having fun on the merry-go-round.

funny

If something is funny, it makes you laugh.

Polly and Jack are laughing at a funny joke.

fur

the soft hair that covers some animals

a cat with soft, white fur

a b c d e f g h i j k l m n o p q r s t u v w x y z

game

something that you play, such as basketball or cards. Games often have rules.

gentle

If you are gentle, you are careful, quiet and kind.

Pip is a gentle dog.

gift

something special that you give to someone or that they give to you

garden

a piece of land near a house, where people grow vegetables and flowers

gerbil

a small, furry animal with long legs. Some people keep gerbils as pets.

giraffe

an African animal that has a very long neck and legs

gas

something that is not solid or liquid, and is very light and invisible like air

This balloon is filled with a gas called helium.

ghost

a person who has died that some people think they can see

girl

a child who is not a boy

gate

a kind of door in a fence, wall or hedge

giant

a very tall person, in a story

give (gave, given)

let someone have something to keep

Ethan is giving Jenny four wagons for her train.

a b c d e f **g** h i j k l m n o p q r s t u v w x y z

glad
pleased and happy

Sally is very glad to
see her friend.

glass
1. something hard and clear
that windows are made from

2. a kind of cup
that is made
from glass

glasses
something that you can
wear on your face to help
you see better

glove
something that you wear on
your hand to keep it warm

glue
a thick liquid that you use to
stick things together

Danny is
gluing down
paper
shapes with
glue.

go (went, been)
move or travel from one
place to another

These cars are going onto
the ship.

goal
when you kick, hit or throw
a ball into a net, in games
such as soccer

GOAL!

goat
a farm animal with a short
tail

gold
a yellow metal that is very
expensive

good (better, best)
1. If something is good, you
like it.

2. done well

good work

3 + 3 = 6 ✓
2 + 5 = 7 ✓
8 − 6 = 2 ✓
4 + 1 = 5 ✓

3. not naughty

goodbye
a word you say when you
go away or someone goes
away from you

Goodbye!

goose (geese)
a large bird with a long neck

a b c d e f g h i j k l m n o p q r s t u v w x y z

grape

a small, soft purple or green fruit that grows in bunches

a bunch of grapes

grapefruit

a large, round fruit with a thick yellow or pink skin

grass

a plant with thin, green leaves. Grass grows in fields and yards.

great

1. big or important

2. very good

We had a great day at the beach.

ground

what you walk on outside

Polly is looking at some ants on the ground.

group

a number of people or things that are together

a group of children

grow (grew, grown)

get bigger

My plant grew very fast.

grown-up

someone who is not a child

Grown-ups are always talking.

guess

try to think of an answer to something that you do not know

Can you guess what's in the box?

guest

someone who comes to visit or stay for a short time

Ellie is welcoming her guests to her party.

guinea pig

a small, furry animal that doesn't have a tail

guitar

a musical instrument with strings

a b c d e f g h i j k l m n o p q r s t u v w x y z

Hh hair *to* hard

hair
the stuff that grows on your head

Rosie has long hair.   Katie has curly hair.

hammer
a tool that you use for knocking nails into something

hang (hung, hung)
put something on a hook, nail or knob

Jack is hanging his coat on a hook.

hairbrush
something you use to brush your hair

hamster
a small, furry animal with a short tail

happen
take place

What is happening in this picture?

half (halves)
one of two pieces of something that are exactly the same size

Each mouse has half of the sandwich.

hand
a part of your body at the end of your arm

happy
If you are happy, you feel pleased about something and not sad.

Sally is feeling very happy today.

hamburger
a round, flat piece of meat that you usually eat on a bun

handle
something you use to hold or move something

hard
1. solid and not soft
2. not easy; difficult

It's hard to put up a tent on hard ground.

a b c d e f g h i j k l m n o p q r s t u v w x y z

35

hat
something that you wear on your head

hear (heard, heard)
take in sounds through your ears

Woof woof!

Jack can hear a dog barking.

height
how tall someone or something is

Dad is checking Milo's height on the chart.

hate
If you hate something, you do not like it at all.

Maddy hates spiders.

heart
1. the thing that pushes blood around your body

My heart is beating fast.

2. a shape

helicopter
a machine that flies. It has blades on top that spin around very fast.

have (had, had)
1. If you have something, it is with you.

Julia has some new red shoes.

2. feel or suffer

Helen has a cold.

heat
make something hot

Yvonne is heating coffee in the microwave.

hello
a word you say when you meet someone

Hello!

head
the part of your body that has your eyes, mouth and ears in it

heavy
hard to lift, push or pull; not light

Thomas and Jack are trying to move a heavy package.

helmet
a hard hat that stops you from hurting your head

Grace wears a helmet for skateboarding.

a b c d e f g **h** i j k l m n o p q r s t u v w x y z

help

do something useful for someone

Jack is helping his dad with the cooking.

hen (also called a chicken)

a bird that farmers keep.

hide (hid, hidden)

1. go to a place where no one can see you

The clown is hiding from Annie.

2. put something in a place where no one can find it

high

1. a long way from the ground

The balloon is high in the sky.

2. going up a long way

highchair

a special chair for babies and small children

hill

a high piece of land. Hills are not as tall as mountains.

hippopotamus

(also called a hippo) a very big animal with short legs and thick skin

hit (hit, hit)

push or knock someone or something very hard

Alice is hitting the ball with her racket.

hold (held, held)

1. have something in your arms or hands

2. have room for something

How many does this hold?

hole

a gap or hollow space in something

There is a hole in this sweater.

home

the place where you live

honey

a sweet, sticky liquid that bees make

a b c d e f g h i j k l m n o p q r s t u v w x y z

hop

jump on one leg

horse

a big animal with four legs and a long tail. People ride horses.

hospital

a building where you go when you are sick or hurt. Doctors and nurses work at hospitals.

hot

very warm; not cold

Don't touch the hot saucepans!

hotdog

a special kind of sausage that you eat in a long, soft bun, with mustard

hotel

a big building with a lot of bedrooms. You can pay to stay there.

hour

an amount of time. There are 60 mintues in an hour and 24 hours in a day.

On a clock, the little hand shows the hours.

house

a building that people live in

hug

put your arms around someone or something and hold them tightly

hungry

If you are hungry, you want to eat something.

Oliver is very hungry.

hurry

do something fast

Jack and Polly are hurrying to catch a bus.

hurt (hurt, hurt)

If something hurts, you feel pain there.

Ross is crying because his tummy hurts.

a b c d e f g **h** i j k l m n o p q r s t u v w x y z

Ii ice *to* itch

ice

water that has frozen solid

ice cubes

ice cream

a very cold, sweet food made from cream or milk

idea

something new that you think of

I know, let's go to the park!

Andy has an idea.

insect

a small animal with six legs

inside

1. in something

This kitten is inside a flowerpot.

2. in a building; indoors

instead

in place of something

Let's have iced tea instead of juice this afternoon.

Internet

millions of computers all over the world linked together. You can use the Internet to find out things.

Polly is using the Internet.

invitation

something that you give someone to ask them to do something with you

Imogen invites Bob to a Jungle Party on Saturday, April 6th at Oxten Community Center at 2:00 RSVP

invite

ask someone to come somewhere or do something

Can you come to my party?

iron

something you use to make your clothes smooth

island

a piece of land with water all around it

itch

If your skin itches, you want to scratch it.

George's ear itches.

a b c d e f g h i j k l m n o p q r s t u v w x y z

jacket

a short coat

Kathy is wearing a yellow jacket.

jar

something that you keep things in. Jars are usually made of glass.

jeans

pants made from a strong material called denim

jigsaw puzzle

a picture cut into pieces. You put the pieces together to make the picture again.

job

1. what someone does to earn money

Aggie has a job as a gardener.

2. something that needs to be done

join

1. become part of a club or group

2. attach two things together

Ethan's going to join the wagons to the train.

joke

something you say to make people laugh

What flowers are between your nose and chin?

Tulips!

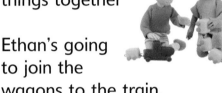

journey

If you go on a journey, you travel from one place to another.

a train journey

juggle

keep two or more things in the air by throwing and catching them, one after the other

juice

liquid that comes from fruit or vegetables

jump

use your legs to push yourself suddenly into the air

jungle

a place in a hot country where many trees and plants grow and many animals live

a b c d e f g h i **j** k l m n o p q r s t u v w x y z

Kk kangaroo *to* kite

kangaroo

a large animal that moves around by jumping

keep (kept, kept)

1. have something and not give it away

Sam keeps his things on a shelf.

2. make something stay the same

key

something you use to unlock a door or to start a car

kick

hit something with your foot

kid

1. a child

2. a young goat

a goat and a kid

kill

make something die

Someone has killed my plant.

kind¹

a type or sort

There are lots of different kinds of fruit.

kind²

If you are kind, you help other people.

Mr. Dot is kind. He does all his neighbor's shopping.

king

a man who rules a country. Kings come from royal families. They are not chosen.

Adam is dressed up as a king.

kiss

touch someone with your lips

kitchen

a room where you make meals

kite

a toy that flies in the wind on the end of a long string

a b c d e f g h i j k l m n o p q r s t u v w x y z

kitten
a young cat

This kitten is playing with a ball of yarn.

knight
a soldier who lived a long time ago. Knights wore armor and rode horses.

ladder
something you can use to climb up to high places

knee
the bony part in the middle of your leg that makes it bend

knock
hit something hard

Pip knocked the chair over.

lady
a woman

These ladies are talking.

kneel (knelt, knelt)
get down on your knees

knot
a place where something, such as string, is tied

ladybug
a small red or yellow insect with black spots

knife (knives)
something you use to cut things. It has a long, sharp edge and a handle.

know (knew, known)
1. If you know someone, you have met them before.

These children know each other.

2. have something in your mind

lake
a big area of water with land around it

a b c d e f g h i j k l m n o p q r s t u v w x y z

lamb
a young sheep

a sheep and a lamb

large
If someone or something is large, they are big.

Becky is standing under a large tree.

lazy
If a person or an animal is lazy, they do not want to do anything.

a lazy cat

lamp
something that makes light

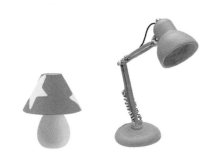

last
1. at the end

The black dog is last.

2. the time before

lead (led, led)
go in front to show the way

This duck is leading her ducklings.

land
the parts of the Earth that are not covered by water

This map shows the land in brown.

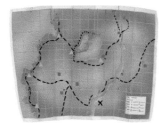

late
1. after the right time

The bus is late again.

2. near the end of something

leaf (leaves)
one of the thin, flat parts of a plant or tree

language
the words that people use to speak and write

Alex and Polly are speaking different languages.

laugh
make sounds that show that you think something is funny

lean (leaned, leaned)
bend to one side

the Leaning Tower of Pisa

a b c d e f g h i j k l m n o p q r s t u v w x y z

l   learn *to* lick

learn (learned, learned)

get to know and understand something you did not know before

Steve is learning to play the guitar.

leave (left, left)

1. go away from a place

Mr. Bun is leaving.

2. let something stay where it is

I left my bag at home.

left

on the side opposite the right side

Lisa is holding the crayon in her left hand.

leg

a part of your body that you use for standing and walking

Tamsin wears tights on her legs.

lemon

a yellow fruit with a thick skin

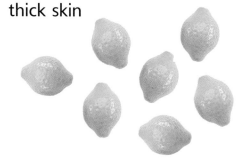

length

how long something is

Use a ruler to measure the length of the paper.

less

not as much

Ethan has less ice cream than Olivia.

lesson

the time when someone teaches you something

$2 + 4 = 6$

let (let, let)

If someone lets you do something, they say that you can do it.

Mr. Dot let Jack mail his letter.

letter

1. something like A, B or Z that you use to make words

2. a message that you write on paper

2244 York Avenue
Tulsa, OK 74146

March 31st

Dear Elizabeth,

Thank you for the lovely bag you gave me. I take it to school every day.

Love, Olivia xxx

lettuce

a vegetable with big leaves that you eat in salads

lick

move your tongue across something

a b c d e f g h i j k l m n o p q r s t u v w x y z

lid

the top of something like a box or jar

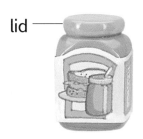

lid

lie¹ (lay, lain)

rest with your body flat on something like a bed

lie²

say something that is not true

Is she in there?

No!

life (lives)

the time when someone or something is alive

Granny and Granddad have had long and happy lives.

lift

pick something up

The clown is lifting a tree out of his bag.

light¹

1. Light comes from the Sun and from lamps. It lets you see.

2. something that gives light, such as a lamp

light²

1. easy to lift, push or pull; not heavy

2. If a color is light, it is pale and not dark.

light pink

like¹

If you like something or someone, you think they are nice.

Becky likes strawberries.

like²

If someone is like another person, they are the same in some way.

Sarah looks a lot like her brother.

line

1. a long, thin mark

2. a group of people or things in a row

a line of soccer players

lion

a big, wild animal with light brown fur

lip

the edge of your mouth

lip

a b c d e f g h i j k l m n o p q r s t u v w x y z

list

words that someone has written down one after the other

long

1. If something is long, one of its ends is far from the other.

A giraffe has a long neck.

2. lasting a lot of time

loud

If someone or something is loud, they make a lot of noise.

Steve's guitar is very loud.

live

1. If you live in a place, that is where your home is.

2. If someone or something lives, they are alive.

look

use your eyes to see something

Polly is looking at the clown.

love

like someone or something very much

Beth loves taking a bath.

lock

something that keeps things like doors and boxes shut. You need a key to open a lock.

a lock

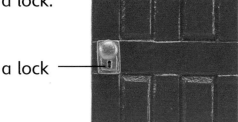

lose (lost, lost)

1. If you lose something, you can't find it.

2. If you lose a game, you don't win it.

Simon and Ian lost.

low

not far from the ground

This bird is flying very low.

log

a big piece of wood that has been cut from a tree

lot

a large amount or number

a lot of bears

lunch

the meal you eat in the middle of the day

Sally is eating pizza for lunch.

a b c d e f g h i j k l m n o p q r s t u v w x y z

Mm machine *to* meal

machine
something with moving parts that work together to do a job

a sewing machine

magic
1. In stories, people use magic to make impossible things happen.

2. clever tricks that look impossible

The clown is doing some magic.

main
the biggest or most important

the main entrance of the museum

make (made, made)
1. put something together

Ethan is making potato people.

2. If you make something happen, it happens because of something you do.

man (men)
a grown-up who is not a woman

Our teacher is a man.

many (more, most)
a large number; a lot of

There are many bees on this flower.

map
a drawing that shows where places are. Maps show roads, rivers and buildings.

market
a place where you can buy things. Markets are often outdoors.

match¹
1. a game that two teams play against each other

a tennis match

2. a small stick that makes fire when you rub its tip against its box

match²
If things match, they are like each other in some way.

These socks match.

These socks don't match.

matter
If something matters, it is important to you.

Winning really matters to Neil and his team.

meal
the food that you eat at special times of the day. Breakfast, lunch and dinner are meals.

a b c d e f g h i j k l m n o p q r s t u v w x y z

mean (meant, meant)

1. If you say what something means, you explain it.

This means that two groups of two equals four.

2. plan to do something

measure

find out how big or heavy something is

meat

a kind of food that comes from animals

medicine

a liquid or pill that you take when you are sick to make you better

meet (met, met)

If you meet someone, you both go to the same place at the same time.

Polly and Lisa met at the fruit stand.

mend

repair something that is broken

Robert is mending his shirt.

mess

untidy and sometimes dirty

What a mess!

message

words that you send or leave for someone when you can't speak to them

Mom!
Paula called about tomorrow.
Call her back.

metal

hard stuff that comes out of the ground. Gold, silver, iron and copper are metals.

This bucket is made of metal.

microwave

a small oven that cooks or heats up food very fast

middle

the place that is the same distance away from all the sides of something

This bear is in the middle of the grass.

milk

a white liquid that you can drink. Milk usually comes from cows.

a b c d e f g h i j k l m n o p q r s t u v w x y z

mind

be worried or unhappy about something

I don't mind spiders.

mistake

If you make a mistake, you do something wrong.

I made a spelling mistake.

monkey

an animal with a long tail and long arms and legs

minute

an amount of time. There are 60 seconds in a minute and 60 minutes in an hour.

It's a few minutes past nine.

mix

put things together to make one thing

Oliver is mixing flour, sugar, eggs, butter and raisins to make a cake.

month

a part of the year that lasts about 4 weeks. There are 12 months in a year.

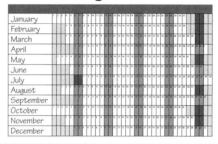

mirror

a special piece of glass that you can see yourself in

model

a small copy of something

Billy is playing with his model ship.

Moon

the big, bright thing that you often see in the sky at night

miss

1. feel unhappy because someone is not with you

Liddy misses her mom.

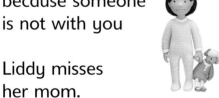

2. not catch a bus or train

money

coins and bills that you use to buy things

more

a bigger number, amount or size

Sally has more sand than Amy.

a b c d e f g h i j k l m n o p q r s t u v w x y z

morning
the part of the day before
12 o'clock (noon)

mountain
a very high piece of land.
Mountains are taller than
hills.

much (more, most)
a big amount

Mrs. Moon
doesn't
have much
to carry.

most
the biggest number or
amount

Which caterpillar has
the most black stripes?

mouse
1. (plural: mice) a small,
furry animal with a
long tail

2. something you
use to move things
around on a
computer screen

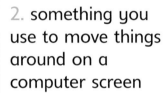

mud
wet earth

Sally is
covered
in mud.

moth
an insect with four large
wings

mouth
the part of your face that
you use to eat and talk

mushroom
a kind of plant that is the
shape of a small umbrella.
You can eat some kinds of
mushrooms.

motorcycle
a big, heavy bicycle with an
engine

move
1. go from one place to
another
2. take something from one
place to another

The crane is moving the box.

music
the sounds that you make
when you sing or play a
musical instrument

a b c d e f g h i j k l m n o p q r s t u v w x y z

Nn nail *to* nest

nail

1. a pointed thing that you use to join pieces of wood together

2. one of the hard parts at the end of your fingers and toes

name

what you call a person or thing

What's your toy's name?

Her name is Tabby.

narrow

If something is narrow, its sides or edges are not far apart.

The gap is too narrow for the kitten to get through.

nature

everything in the world, such as plants and animals, not made by people

naughty

If you are naughty, you do things that you are not meant to do.

Naughty Pip has stolen a piece of Jack's cake.

near

not far away; close

The school is near the river.

neck

the part of your body that joins your head to your shoulders

A giraffe has a very long neck.

necklace

something pretty that you wear around your neck

need

If you need something, you must have it.

Sam needs sleep.

needle

1. a thin, pointed piece of metal that you use for sewing

2. a long metal or plastic stick that you use for knitting

neighbor

someone who lives near you

The people who live in these two houses are neighbors.

nest

a home made by birds and some other animals. Birds lay their eggs in nests.

a b c d e f g h i j k l m **n** o p q r s t u v w x y z

net[1]

1. a kind of bag that you use to catch fish and other animals

2. the thing you hit balls over in games such as tennis

Net[2]

a short name for the Internet

Polly is using the Net.

never

not at any time

The grumpy mailman never smiles.

new

1. just made, bought or born

Julia has new shoes.

2. different

a new school

news

information about things that have happened in your life or in the world

Mrs. Beef has some sad news.

I've lost my cat!

newspaper

big sheets of paper with stories and pictures about the news

next

1. the one after this

2. nearest to; beside

The red car is next to a yellow car.

nice

If you think something is nice, you like it.

Danny has made a nice picture.

night

the time when it is dark outside and people sleep

nod

move your head up and down

The dog is nodding.

noise

a sound that someone or something makes

The baby is making lots of noise.

WAAAH!

noisy

very loud

The boys are being very noisy.

a b c d e f g h i j k l m n o p q r s t u v w x y z

nose

the part of your face that you use to smell and breathe

note

1. a sound that you make when you sing or play music

a high note

2. a short message that you write

Remember to feed the cat!

notebook

a book with clean pages for you to write on

notice

see something and pay attention to it

Annie hasn't noticed the clown.

now

at this time

The clown takes a pie out of his bag...

...now he trips.

number

a word or sign that shows how many

1   7   88   1,200
three   twenty-two
one hundred

nurse

someone who takes care of people who are sick or hurt

nut

something with a hard shell. Many kinds of nuts are good to eat.

ocean

a very large sea

o'clock

a word you use when you say what time it is

It's seven o'clock.

octopus

a sea animal with eight long arms

odd

1. An odd number is a number that you can't divide by two.

The bunny is jumping on odd numbers.

1   2   3   4   5

2. strange or unusual

a b c d e f g h i j k l m n o p q r s t u v w x y z

often

If you do something often, you do it a lot.

Mr. Dot and Jack often do the shopping.

oil

a thick liquid. Some oil is used to make machines work or to make heat. Some oil from plants is used for cooking.

cooking oil

old

1. If someone or something is old, they have lived for a long time.

2. made or bought some time ago

an old shoe

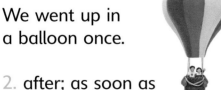

once

1. only one time

We went up in a balloon once.

2. after; as soon as

You can watch TV once you've done your homework.

onion

a round vegetable with papery skin and a strong smell and taste

only

and no more; just

Becky only has two strawberries.

open¹

1. move something such as a door so that you can go through it

2. take the lid off something

Mrs. Dot is opening the box.

open²

If something is open, you can go through it or into it.

The pet store is open all day.

opposite¹

The opposite of something is the thing that is the most different from it.

Big is the opposite of small.

opposite²

If two things or people are opposite each other, they are facing each other.

Becky is sitting opposite the teddy bear.

orange

1. a round, juicy fruit with a thick skin

2. a color

other

1. different

Do you have any other toys?

No, just cars.

2. one of two
Where's your other shoe?

a b c d e f g h i j k l m n o p q r s t u v w x y z

Pp

outside
1. not inside a building

Let's go outside!

2. not in something

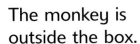

The monkey is outside the box.

over
1. on top of

The bird is flying over the tree.

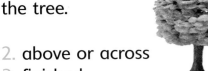

2. above or across
3. finished
4. down

owl
a bird with big eyes. Owls catch small animals at night.

own
If you own something, it is yours.

Mrs. Bird owns a pet store.

page
a piece of paper attached inside a book

Turn the page.

paint[1]
a special liquid that you use to put color on things

jugs of paint

paint[2]
1. use a brush and paints to make a picture

2. put paint on something to change its color

pair
the name for two things that go together

a pair of socks

palace
a very large house where kings, queens, princes and princesses live

pale
If a color is pale, it is very light.

pale blue

pale green

pale yellow

paper
1. something that you write, draw and paint on

2. short for newspaper

parachute
a large piece of cloth that can carry people safely to the ground from a plane

a b c d e f g h i j k l m n o p q r s t u v w x y z

parent

a mother or father

Mr. and Mrs. Dot are Polly and Jack's parents.

park[1]

a big piece of land where people can walk and play

park[2]

leave a car somewhere

Jan and Jo are going to park in the parking lot.

parrot

a bird with bright feathers and a curved beak

part

something that belongs to something bigger

A wheel is part of a car.

party

when a group of friends meet to eat, drink and have fun together

a costume party

pass

1. go past someone or something

passing the bank

2. give something to someone when they can't reach it

3. do well in a test or exam

past[1]

the time that has gone

This is how some people dressed in the past.

past[2]

by or beside

The children and dogs are running past the pet store.

path

a small road for people to walk or ride on

paw

an animal's foot

a tiger's paw

pay

give someone money for something

Ethan is paying for an apple.

a b c d e f g h i j k l m n o p q r s t u v w x y z

pea

a very small, green, round vegetable

pear

a juicy green or yellow fruit

penguin

a black and white bird that lives in cold places

peach

a soft, round fruit with a furry skin

pebble

a smooth, round stone. You find pebbles on beaches.

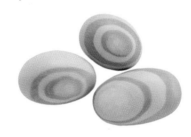

people

men, women and children

There are seven people here.

peak

1. the very top of a mountain

2. the round, front part of a cap

peak

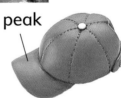

pen

a metal or plastic thing that you use to write or draw in ink

pepper

1. a black or gray powder you can put on food to add flavor.

2. a type of vegetable

peanut

a small, oval nut. Peanuts are often roasted before you eat them.

pencil

a long, thin piece of wood with a black stick in the middle that you use for writing and drawing

person

a man, woman or child

This person is a builder.

a b c d e f g h i j k l m n o p q r s t u v w x y z

pet
an animal that you keep at home

phone (short for telephone)
something you use to talk to someone in another place

photograph
a picture that you take with a camera

Polly is looking at photographs.

piano
a musical instrument with black and white keys that you tap with your fingers

pick
1. choose something

2. take fruit or flowers from a tree or plant

picnic
a meal that you take to eat outdoors

picture
a painting, drawing or photograph

piece
a part of something

pillow
something that you rest your head on when you are lying in bed

pilot
someone who flies a plane

Jim wants to be a pilot when he grows up.

pineapple
a large yellow or brown fruit, with pointed leaves at the top

pizza
a flat, round piece of bread with tomatoes, cheese and other food on top

a b c d e f g h i j k l m n o **p** q r s t u v w x y z

place

somewhere such as a building, country or town. It can be very big or small.

a good place for a snack

planet

an enormous, round thing that goes around the Sun. The Earth is a planet.

playground

a place where you can play outdoors

plan¹

a map of a building or a place

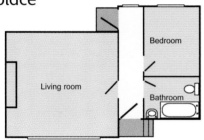

plant

a living thing that grows in soil or in water. Trees and flowers are plants.

please

a word that you say when you ask for something in a polite way

Could I please have some more strawberries?

plan²

decide how to do something

1. Decide date
2. Send out invitations
3. Buy food and drink
   Decorate the house

Mrs. Dot is planning a party.

plate

a round, flat thing that you put food on

plum

a small, soft fruit with red, purple or yellow skin

plane (short for airplane)

a big machine that flies

play

1. do something for fun

2. use a musical instrument to make music

3. take part in a sport

pocket

a small bag that is part of your clothes. You can keep things in your pockets.

Renata is putting her hands in her pockets.

a b c d e f g h i j k l m n o p q r s t u v w x y z

poem

a piece of writing. Poems usually have short lines and may have words that rhyme.

My Cat
My cat is sitting in the sun,
While I am having lots of fun.
My cat is sleeping in the house,
And dreaming that she's caught a mouse.

by Polly Dot

police car

a special car that the police use for their work

poor

1. If you are poor, you don't have much money.

2. a word you use when you feel sorry for someone

Poor Ross, his tummy hurts.

point¹

1. the sharp end of something

the point of a pencil

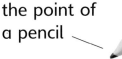

2. part of the score in a game

I have three points now.

pond

a small area of water

potato

a white, red or brown vegetable that grows under the ground

point²

use your finger to show where something is

Polly is pointing to Jack's nose.

pony

a small horse

present

something special that you give to someone or that they give to you

police

The police are people whose job is to stop people from breaking the law.

pool

a place where people go to swim or play in the water

press

push something

Danny is pressing down the blue paper to make the sea.

a b c d e f g h i j k l m n o **p** q r s t u v w x y z

pretend

act as if something is true when it is not

pretending to be asleep

pretty

nice to look at

Anya is wearing a pretty red dress.

price

how much money something costs

2 for the price of 1

prince

the son of a king or queen

princess

the daughter of a king or queen or the wife of a prince

prize

something that you win when you do well

promise

say that you will really do something

I promise I'll take you to the park.

puddle

a small pool of water on the ground that you see after it has been raining

pull

move someone or something toward you

Thomas   Jack

Jack is pulling the big package.

pumpkin

a very big, round fruit with a hard orange or yellow skin

pupil

someone who is learning something, usually in a school

a photo of Mr. Levy and some of his pupils

puppet

a kind of doll that you make move

a b c d e f g h i j k l m n o p q r s t u v w x y z

puppy

a young dog

a puppy and a dog

push

move someone or something away from you

Thomas is pushing the big package.

Thomas   Jack

put (put, put)

move something to a place

Oliver is putting a bottle of green paint on the table.

puzzle

a game that you have to think about very carefully

quack

When a duck quacks, it opens its beak and makes a loud sound.

Quack! Quack!

quarter

one of four pieces of something that are the same size

a quarter

queen

a woman who rules a country. Queens are not chosen.

Joy is dressed up as a queen.

question

what you say or write when you want to find out something

What's your name?

quick

1. If someone or something is quick, they move very fast.

2. lasting only a short time

quiet

not making much noise

You need to be very quiet to creep up on someone.

quite

1. fairly or rather

I'm quite tired.

2. completely

Mr. Bun hasn't quite finished all his baking.

quiz

a kind of game where you have to answer questions

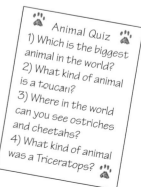

Animal Quiz
1) Which is the biggest animal in the world?
2) What kind of animal is a toucan?
3) Where in the world can you see ostriches and cheetahs?
4) What kind of animal was a Triceratops?

a b c d e f g h i j k l m n o p q r s t u v w x y z

rabbit

a furry animal with long ears and a short tail

rainbow

a curved band of different colors that you sometimes see in the sky

reach

1. stretch out your hand to touch something

The firefighter is reaching out to rescue the cat.

2. arrive at a place

race

a competition to find out who is the fastest

raisin

a small, dried grape that you can eat as a snack or in muffins

read (read, read)

look at words and understand what they mean

radio

a machine that plays music and programs that you can listen to

raspberry

a small, soft, red fruit

ready

If you are ready, you can do something immediately.

These children are ready to swim.

rain

If it rains, drops of water fall down from the sky.

rat

a small animal with a long tail and sharp teeth

real

1. not a copy

Is that fruit real or plastic?

2. true

I like real adventure stories.

a b c d e f g h i j k l m n o p q **r** s t u v w x y z

recorder
a musical instrument that you blow into

refrigerator
a kind of metal cupboard that keeps food cold

remember
bring something into your mind again

Fiona can remember the order of the colors of the rainbow.

red, orange, yellow, green, blue, indigo, violet

reply
give an answer

Do you want to go to the park?

Yes please.

Minnie is replying to her dad's question.

rescue
help someone or something escape from danger

rhinoceros
(also called a rhino)
a very big animal with thick skin and horns on its nose

ribbon
a long, thin piece of cloth that you tie around things

Becky has green ribbons in her hair.

rice
a food that comes from a kind of grass plant. You cook and eat grains of rice.

rich
If you are rich, you have a lot of money.

a rich popstar

ride (rode, ridden)
sit on a bicycle or horse and move along

right
1. without any mistakes in it

That's the right answer.

2. the side opposite the left side

The puppet is on Greta's right hand.

ring¹
1. something pretty that you wear around your finger

2. a circle with a hole in the middle

a b c d e f g h i j k l m n o p q r s t u v w x y z

ring² (rang, rung)

When a bell or telephone rings, it makes a loud noise.

The phone's ringing.

robot

a machine that can do some of the things that people do

a toy robot

room

1. a space inside a building with walls around it

This plan shows six rooms.

2. space

Is there any room for me?

ripe

If fruit is ripe, it is soft and ready to eat.

rock

1. a very big stone

2. a kind of music with a strong beat

Steve likes to play rock music.

rope

something made of lots of strong threads twisted together. You can use a rope for pulling heavy things.

river

a wide line of water that flows across land to the sea

These houses are near the river.

rocket

a machine that takes astronauts into space. Rockets travel very fast.

a toy rocket

rose

a flower with a prickly stem. Many roses smell nice.

road

a hard piece of ground that goes from one place to another

roof

the part of a building that keeps the rain out

roof

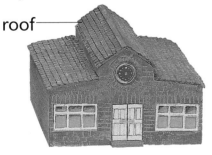

round

shaped like a circle or ball

Drums are usually round.

a b c d e f g h i j k l m n o p q r s t u v w x y z

rug

something that covers part of a floor

ruler

a flat piece of plastic, wood or metal that you use to measure things and draw straight lines.

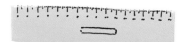

run (ran, run)

move quickly using your legs

rush

do something quickly; hurry

Jack, Polly and the dogs are rushing past the post office.

sad

not happy

saddle

a seat for a rider on a horse

saddle

safe

1. If you are safe, you are not in danger.
2. If something is safe, it can't hurt you.

a safe place to cross

sailor

someone who works on a ship

salad

a mixture of uncooked food, such as lettuce and tomatoes

salami

a kind of big sausage with a strong flavor. You usually eat thin slices of salami.

salt

a white powder that you put on food or use in cooking to add flavor

same

If two things or people are the same, they are just like each other.

The twins always wear the same clothes.

a b c d e f g h i j k l m n o p q r s t u v w x y z

sand

a powder made of tiny pieces of rock and shell. It covers some beaches and deserts.

sandal

a kind of shoe that you wear when it is hot

sandwich

two pieces of bread with another kind of food between them

saucer

a small plate that you put under a cup

a cup and saucer

sausage

something that you eat made from chopped meat put into a special skin

save

1. rescue someone or something from danger

2. keep money to spend later

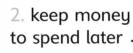

Jack saves coins in this cow money bank.

saw

a tool that you use to cut wood

say (said, said)

speak words

There was an old woman who lived in a shoe...

scarf

a long thing that you wear around your neck to keep warm

school

a place where children go to learn

scissors

something you use to cut paper or cloth

scooter

a small machine that you can push along with one foot

a b c d e f g h i j k l m n o p q r s t u v w x y z

sea

a very large area of salty water

seal

an animal with smooth fur that lives in the sea and on land

search

look carefully for something

Annie, Megan and Tim are searching for their friend.

seat

a place where you can sit

secret

something that only a few people know

Amy is telling Anna a secret.

see (saw, seen)

1. use your eyes to look at something

Can you see the clown?

2. meet someone

I'll see you on Monday.

sell (sold, sold)

let someone have something if they give you money

Mrs. Hussain is selling Ethan an apple.

send (sent, sent)

make something or someone go somewhere

Jack is sending a letter to his friend.

sentence

a group of words that makes sense. A sentence starts with a capital letter and ends with a period.

My dad likes apples.

a sentence

sew (sewed, sewn)

connect pieces of cloth together using a needle and thread

shadow

a dark shape that is made by something getting in the way of light

shake (shook, shaken)

move something up and down or from side to side

Anton loves to shake his rattle.

a b c d e f g h i j k l m n o p q r **s** t u v w x y z

shallow

not going down very far; not very deep

The wading pool is shallow.

shampoo

a liquid that you use when you wash your hair

share

let someone have a part of something or use something with you

Bill is sharing his cherries with Ben.

shark

a big fish with sharp teeth

sharp

If something is sharp, it has a very thin edge or a point that can cut or prick you.

a sharp pencil

sheep (sheep)

a farm animal with a wooly coat. Most wool comes from sheep.

sheet

1. a big piece of cloth that you put on a bed

2. a flat piece of paper, glass or plastic

shelf (shelves)

a long, flat piece of wood, metal or plastic that is attached to a wall

shell

1. the hard cover around some sea animals and snails

2. the hard part around eggs and nuts

ship

a very big boat that carries people and things over the sea

shirt

something that you wear on the top part of your body. A shirt often has buttons down the front.

shoe

something you wear to cover your foot

a b c d e f g h i j k l m n o p q r s t u v w x y z

short

1. not very long

Maisie has short hair.

2. not tall

Minnie is short for her age.

shorts

pants with short legs

shoulder

a part of your body between your neck and your arm

Jack's shoulder

shout

talk very loudly

COME BACK PIP!

show (showed, shown)

1. let someone see something

Jack is showing Thomas his hands.

2. explain how to do something by doing it yourself

shower

1. something you use to wash yourself

2. a short fall of rain

shrink (shrank, shrunk)

get smaller

This pink sweater shrank in the wash.

shut (shut, shut)

move a door or cover to block a space or opening; close

Danny is shutting the door of the playhouse.

side

1. the edge of something

2. a flat surface of something

A piece of paper has two sides.

3. a team

sign¹

1. words or pictures that tell you what to do

a road sign

2. a shape that means something

@ is the sign for "at".

sign²

write your name on something

Sign here please.

since

from that time

They've been waiting for the bus since 2:30.

a b c d e f g h i j k l m n o p q r **s** t u v w x y z

sing (sang, sung)

use your voice to make music

sink¹

something that you wash things in. Sinks have faucets and a plug.

sink² (sank, sunk)

go downward underwater

sit (sat, sat)

put your bottom on something and rest

size

how big or small something is

skate

move smoothly on ice wearing special boots called skates

ski

travel on snow wearing two long things called skis on your feet

skin

1. the cover of your body

Babies have smooth skin.

2. the outside layer of a fruit or vegetable

skirt

something that girls and women wear

sky

the space above the ground where you can see clouds, stars and planes

sleep (slept, slept)

close your eyes and rest your whole body, usually at night

sleeve

a part of a shirt, top, coat, or sweater that covers your arms

a b c d e f g h i j k l m n o p q r s t u v w x y z

slice

a piece of food that has been cut from a larger piece

slide[1]

something you can play on in a playground

slide[2] (slid, slid)

move smoothly over or down something

slip

slide and fall over

slipper

a soft shoe that you wear indoors

slow

If someone or something is slow, they take a long time to go somewhere or do something; not fast.

a slow train

slowly

If you do something slowly, it takes a long time.

Sally is riding slowly so that she doesn't spill any sand.

slug

a small, soft animal with no legs, like a snail without a shell

small

not big, large or tall; little

Asha is a small child.

smell (smelled, smelled)

1. use your nose to sense something

2. If something smells, you can sense it with your nose.

Your cat smells horrible!

smile

turn up the corners of your mouth to show that you are happy

smooth

If something is smooth, it does not have bumps or lumps in it.

The roller is making the road smooth.

a b c d e f g h i j k l m n o p q r s t u v w x y z

snail

a small, soft animal with no legs and a shell on its back

snake

a long, thin animal with no legs. Some snakes have a poisonous bite.

snow

small, white pieces of ice that fall from the sky when it is very cold

soap

something you use to wash yourself

soccer

a game where two teams try to kick a ball into a net

sock

something you wear on your foot under your shoe

sofa

a long, soft chair for two or more people

soft

not hard or firm

This cat has soft fur.

soil

the earth that plants grow in

soldier

someone whose job is to fight

song

a piece of music with words that you sing

I love you baby... boom ba, boom ba

Natalie is singing a song.

soon

happening not long from now

It will soon be 2 o'clock.

a b c d e f g h i j k l m n o p q r s t u v w x y z

sort

a kind or type

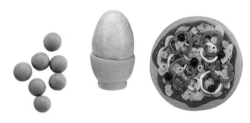

different sorts of food

sound

something that you hear

Squawk!

Parrots make
a squawking
sound.

soup

a liquid food made from
meat or vegetables and
water

space

1. an empty place or area

2. everything outside the
Earth, including the stars
and planets

spacecraft

something that travels into
space from the Earth

speak (spoke, spoken)

say something

How are
you?

I'm fine.

special

1. important or better
than usual

2. made for a
particular job

Electricians need
special tools.

spell¹

In stories, a spell is
special words
or a recipe
that makes
things
change or
happen.

spell² (spelled, spelled)

write or say the letters
of a word in the right order

HARRY

spend (spent, spent)

use money to buy things

Danny is
thinking about
how to spend
his money.

spider

a small animal with eight
legs

spill (spilled, spilled)

let liquid fall out of a
container by mistake

a b c d e f g h i j k l m n o p q r s t u v w x y z

spinach

a vegetable with dark green leaves

splash

throw liquid around

sponge

something you can use for cleaning things or soaking up liquid

spoon

something you use for stirring things and for eating

sport

a kind of game that you play to get exercise and have fun

spot¹

a small, round mark

a dog with black spots

spot²

notice something

Can you spot a clown in this picture?

squirrel

a small animal with a big, furry tail

stairs

a group of steps inside a building

stamp

a small piece of paper with a picture on it that shows you have paid to mail something

Oliver Muncher
233 Grub Avenue
Tulsa, OK 74146

stand (stood, stood)

be upright on your feet

star

1. a little bright light you can see in the sky at night

2. a shape with points

3. a famous person

a movie star

a b c d e f g h i j k l m n o p q r s t u v w x y z

start

do the first part of something; begin

The birds are starting to eat the seeds.

station

a place where people get on or off trains

stay

1. not leave a place

The cows stay in the field all day.

2. live somewhere for a short time

steep

If a hill is steep, it slopes a lot and is hard to climb.

stick[1]

a long, thin piece of wood

stick[2] (stuck, stuck)

use glue to join something onto something else.

still[1]

If someone or something is still, they are not moving at all.

Milo is standing very still.

still[2]

If something is still happening or is still there, it has not stopped or gone.

Oliver ate one apple...

...but he still has some left.

sting (stung, stung)

If an animal or plant stings you, it pricks you and leaves some poison in your body.

Flora is afraid the bee will sting her.

stir

move something around with a spoon or stick

stone

a small rock

stool

a seat without a back

a b c d e f g h i j k l m n o p q r s t u v w x y z

stop

1. not move any more

Jan and Jo stopped at the gate to take a ticket.

2. not happen any more

storm

a strong wind with lots of rain or snow

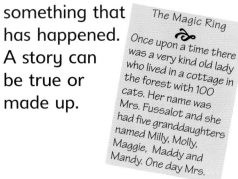

story

words which tell you about something that has happened. A story can be true or made up.

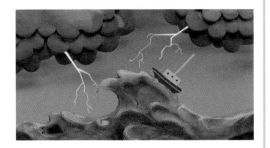

straight

If something is straight, it does not bend or curve.

Leslie has straight hair.

strawberry

a soft, red fruit with tiny seeds on its skin

street

a road in a town or city which usually has buildings on both sides

string

very thin rope that you use to tie things together

strong

1. able to lift heavy things

2. If something is strong, it does not break easily.

3. with a lot of flavor

strong coffee

study¹

a room for reading, writing or working on a computer

study²

learn about something

suddenly

If something happens suddenly, it happens quickly and when you don't expect it.

Suddenly she dropped the vase.

sugar

sweet, white or brown stuff that you can put in drinks or in food

a b c d e f g h i j k l m n o p q r s t u v w x y z

suitcase

a kind of strong bag for carrying clothes and other things

sum

a math question using numbers

$$8 + 2 =$$
$$4 - 2 =$$
$$10 \times 4 =$$

Sun

the very large, bright thing that you see in the sky in the daytime

sunflower

a very tall flower with yellow petals

sunglasses

something that you can wear on your face to shade your eyes from the Sun

supermarket

a big store that sells food and other things

sure

If you are sure about something, you know it is true or right.

Dad isn't sure if they've got everything on the list.

surprise

something that you do not expect

BOO!

It was a surprise when the clown jumped out.

swan

a big white or black bird with a long neck

sweep (swept, swept)

use a broom to clean the floor or ground

sweet

1. lovely; cute

a sweet kitten

2. kind

3. If food is sweet, it has the taste of sugar.

swim (swam, swum)

move through water using your arms and legs

a b c d e f g h i j k l m n o p q r s t u v w x y z

swimming pool

a place made for people to swim in

swimsuit

special clothes that you wear for swimming

swing[1]

something you can sit on in a playground to go backward and forward

swing[2] (swung, swung)

move backward and forward on something that is hanging

table

a piece of furniture with a flat top and legs

tail

the part at the end of some animals' bodies

tail

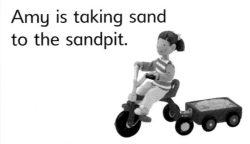

take (took, taken)

1. move or carry something

Amy is taking sand to the sandpit.

2. steal something

talk

speak to people

tall

If someone or something is tall, their head or top is high above the ground.

taste

put food or drink in your mouth to find out what it's like

taxi

a car that you can pay to ride in

tea

a drink made from hot water and dried leaves from a tea plant

a tea bag

a b c d e f g h i j k l m n o p q r s t u v w x y z

teacher
someone whose job is to teach other people

team
a group of people who work or play sports together

teddy bear
a soft, furry toy that looks like a bear

telephone
(also called a phone) something you use to talk to someone in another place

television
(also called a TV) something that shows moving pictures and sends out sounds

tell (told, told)
1. talk to someone about something

Mrs. Beef is telling them about her cat.

2. say that someone must do something

tent
a kind of small house made from strong cloth that you can sleep in outside

thank
tell someone that you are pleased with something they have done or given you

Polly is thanking Marco for the present.

thin
1. not wide; narrow

2. not weighing much; not fat

a thin cat

thing
anything you can see, touch, do or think about

There are lots of things on the table, but Tina still has a few things to do.

think (thought, thought)
1. use your mind

2. believe something

Maddy thinks spiders are scary.

thirsty
If you are thirsty, you want to drink something.

a b c d e f g h i j k l m n o p q r s **t** u v w x y z

through
from one side to the other

Mr. Bun went out through the door.

tie
hold things together with a string, rope or ribbon

Someone has tied the ribbons together.

tip
the very end part of something

This fox's tail has a white tip.

throw (threw, thrown)
make something move through the air

Anna is going to throw the ball.

tiger
a big, wild animal with orange fur and black stripes

toast
a piece of bread which has been cooked until it turns brown

thumb
the shortest of your five fingers, at the side of your hand

time
1. a moment shown on a clock or watch

2. how long something takes to happen

toddler
a young child who is just beginning to walk

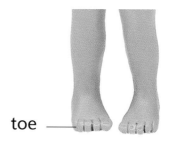

ticket
a small piece of paper that shows you have paid for something

tiny
very small

a small cat   a tiny cat

toe
one of the five parts on the end of your foot

toe ———

a b c d e f g h i j k l m n o p q r s t u v w x y z

together

with another person or thing

Jenny and Ethan are playing together.

tonight

the night or evening of this day

I'm going to a party tonight.

top

1. the highest part of something

The kitten is on the top of the desk.

2. something that you wear on the upper part of your body

toilet

a special bowl with a seat where you go to the bathroom

tooth (teeth)

one of <u>the hard white things</u> <u>inside your mouth</u> that you use for biting and chewing

touch

1. feel something with part of your body

2. If things touch, they are so close there is no space between them.

Please do not touch!

tomato

a soft, juicy red fruit that you eat in salads

toothbrush

a brush that you use for cleaning your teeth

towel

a big piece of thick, soft cloth that you use to dry yourself

tongue

the long, soft part inside your mouth that you use for tasting, eating and talking

toothpaste

a thick liquid that you put on a toothbrush to clean your teeth

town

a place with lots of roads and buildings where many people live and work

a b c d e f g h i j k l m n o p q r s t u v w x y z

toy

something that you play with

tractor

a big thing with large back wheels. Farmers use tractors to pull other machines or heavy loads.

train

a very big thing that can carry a lot of people along on rails

tree

a very large plant with leaves, branches and a trunk

truck

a big thing with wheels that carries things from one place to another

true

1. correct or right

TRUE OR FALSE?
A. An aardvark is a plant.
B. Penguins can't fly.
C. Tadpoles turn into butterflies.

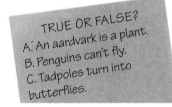

2. If a story is true, it really happened.

try

1. work hard to do something you want to do

They are trying to move the package.

2. test something

T-shirt

something with short sleeves that you wear on the top part of your body

turkey

1. a big bird that farmers keep

2. a kind of meat that comes from a turkey

turn

1. go in a different direction

They are going to turn left.

2. move around

TV

(short for television) something that shows moving pictures and sends out sounds

twin

Twins are two children who have the same mother and were born on the same day. Some twins look alike.

a b c d e f g h i j k l m n o p q r s t u v w x y z

ugly
not pretty to look at

undress
take your clothes off

upside down
with the part that is usually at the top at the bottom

umbrella
something you hold over your head to keep the rain off

unhappy
sad or upset

use
do a job with something

Mr. Clack is using a saw.

under
If something is under something else, it is lower than it.

The kitten is under the wooden boards.

upright
standing straight

useful
If something is useful, it helps you do something.

A wheelbarrow is useful for moving things.

understand
(understood, understood)
know what something means or how it works

Can you understand what Ben is saying?

Ben want dwink!

upset
not happy; angry

Mrs. Beef is upset because she has lost her cat.

usually
If something usually happens, it almost always happens.

Sara usually cycles to school.

a b c d e f g h i j k l m n o p q r s t u v w x y z

Vv vacuum cleaner *to* voice

Ww wait *to* wake

vacuum cleaner
a machine that you use to clean carpets

vase
something you can put flowers in

vegetable
a plant that you can eat

very
You use the word "very" before another word to make it stronger.

dirty   very dirty

view
what you can see from a particular place

visit
go to see someone or something for a short time

The children are going to visit the museum.

visitor
someone who goes to a place to see someone or something

Polly has some visitors.

voice
the sound you make when you talk, shout or sing

LAAAAA!

wait
stay in a place until something happens

waiter
a man who brings the food and drink in a café or restaurant

waitress
a woman who brings the food and drink in a café or restaurant

wake (woke, woken)
stop sleeping

a b c d e f g h i j k l m n o p q r s t u v w x y z

walk

put one foot in front of the other to move along

wall

1. one side of a room or building

2. something made of stone or brick that divides land

want

If you want something, you need it or would like it.

Jenny wants some more wagons for her train.

warm

1. fairly hot

a warm day

2. making you feel fairly hot

a warm coat

wash

use soap and water to make someone or something clean

washing machine

a machine that washes clothes

watch[1]

a small clock that you wear on your wrist

watch[2]

look at someone or something to see what happens

water

the clear liquid that falls as rain and comes out of faucets

Becky is playing in the water.

wave[1]

a big hill of water in the sea

wave[2]

move your hand from side to side to say hello or goodbye

way

1. how you do something

2. how you get from one place to another

This is the way to the village.

a b c d e f g h i j k l m n o p q r s t u v w x y z

wear (wore, worn)
When you wear clothes, they cover your body.

Miriam is wearing a red suit.

well
1. If you are well, you are healthy.

2. If you do something well, you are good at it.

Sarah can read very well now.

while
at the same time as something else is happening

Jack ate a cake while no one was looking.

weather
what it is like outside, for example windy, rainy, sunny or snowy

cold weather

wet
full of water or covered in water

wide
measuring a lot from one side to the other; not narrow

This sofa is wide enough for three cats.

web
1. a thin net that a spider makes to catch insects

2. Web the part of the Internet that you can use to find out information

whale
a very big animal that lives in the sea

wild
not looked after by people; not tame

wild animals

week
A week is seven days. There are 52 weeks in a year.

wheel
a round thing that can turn around

win (won, won)
come first in a game, race or competition

The pink cake won first prize.

a b c d e f g h i j k l m n o p q r s t u v w x y z

wind
air that moves quickly

The wind
blew Alison's
hat off.

window
something in a wall or in a
car that lets in light. There is
usually glass in a window.

wish
something you want to
happen very
much

This fairy can give
you three wishes.

witch
a woman in a story
who can do
magic spells

with
1. If you are with someone,
you are together.

2. using
Draw with a pencil.

3. that has or who has

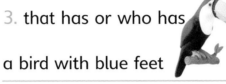

a bird with blue feet

woman (women)
a grown-up who is not a
man; a lady

wood
the hard part of a tree that
can be burned or used to
make things

a table made
of wood

word
a group of sounds or letters
that means something. You
use words
to speak
and write.

a list of
words

work
1. do a job or something
that needs to be done

Mick works
as a builder.

2. If something works, it
does what it should do.

world
the planet that we live on

write (wrote, written)
use a pen or pencil to put
letters or words on
something

Harry has
written his
name.

HARRY

wrong
1. not correct or right

All these
answers
are wrong.

2 + 3 = 7   X
4 + 6 = 9   X
5 - 3 = 1   X

2. naughty or bad

a b c d e f g h i j k l m n o p q r s t u v w x y z

Xx
x *to* xylophone

x

1. You write x after your name to send someone a kiss.

Lots of love from Kathy xxx

2. times or multiplied by

$$2 \times 2 = 4$$

Xmas

a short way of writing "Christmas"

Happy Xmas!

x-ray

a kind of photograph that shows the inside of someone's body

xylophone

a musical instrument with a row of wooden or metal bars. You play it by hitting the bars with special sticks.

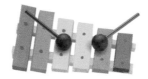

Yy
yawn *to* young

yawn

open your mouth and breathe in deeply because you are tired

year

A year is 12 months.

Freya is five years old. Annie is six years old.

yet

up to this time

Ben can't walk yet.

young

If someone or something is young, they have only lived a short time.

young children

Zz
zebra *to* zoo

zebra

an animal that looks like a horse with black and white stripes

zero

the name for the number 0; nothing

$$5 - 5 = 0$$

Five take away five equals zero.

zipper

something that you use to fasten clothes and bags

zoo

a place where wild animals are kept so that people can go to see them

We saw a panda at the zoo.

a b c d e f g h i j k l m n o p q r s t u v w x y z

Colors

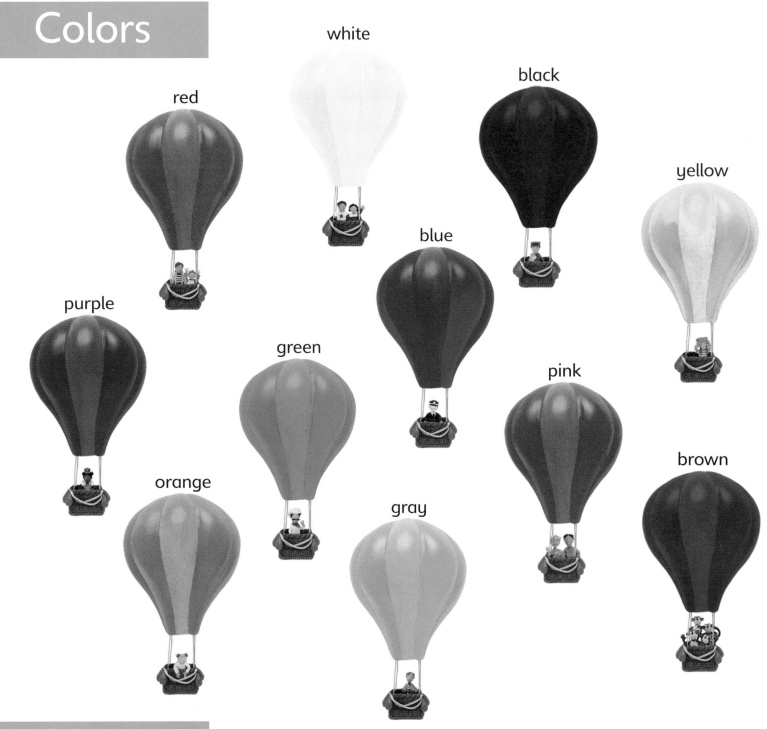

white

red

black

yellow

blue

purple

green

pink

orange

gray

brown

Shapes

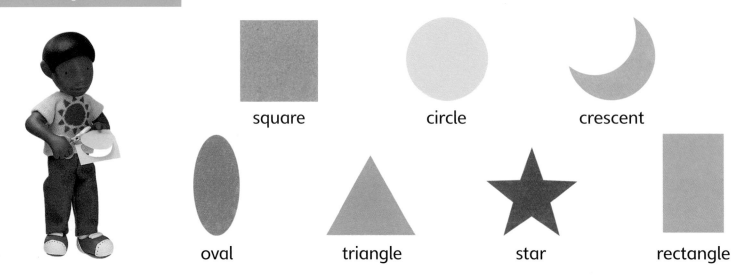

square

circle

crescent

oval

triangle

star

rectangle

Numbers

first	second	third	fourth	fifth	sixth	seventh	eighth	ninth	tenth
1st	2nd	3rd	4th	5th	6th	7th	8th	9th	10th

1 one

2 two

3 three

4 four

5 five

6 six

7 seven

8 eight

9 nine

10 ten

11 eleven

12 twelve

13 thirteen

14 fourteen

15 fifteen

16 sixteen

17 seventeen

18 eighteen

19 nineteen

20 twenty

30	40	50	60	70	80	90	100	1000
thirty	forty	fifty	sixty	seventy	eighty	ninety	hundred	thousand

Days and months

Monday

Tuesday

Wednesday

Thursday

Friday

Saturday

Sunday

January

February

March

April

May

June

July

August

September

October

November

December

Polly's birthday is in January. When is your birthday?

Seasons

Spring

Summer

Fall

Winter

Family words

Polly is looking at some photographs of her family.

Polly and Jack are sister and brother.

Here are Polly's parents. She calls her mother "Mom" or "Mommy". She calls her father "Dad" or "Daddy".

Jack is his parents' son.

Polly is her parents' daughter.

Here are Polly and Jack with their grandparents. Polly calls her grandmother "Granny". She calls her grandfather "Granddad". What do you call yours?

Here's Daddy with his brother Howard.

Here's Jack when he was a baby.

Howard is Polly's uncle. His wife, Kathy, is Polly's aunt. Their little girl is Polly's cousin Aimee.

Polly and Jack are their parents' children. They are their grandparents' grandchildren. Polly is their granddaughter. Jack is their grandson.